Ups

My Life With and

Downs

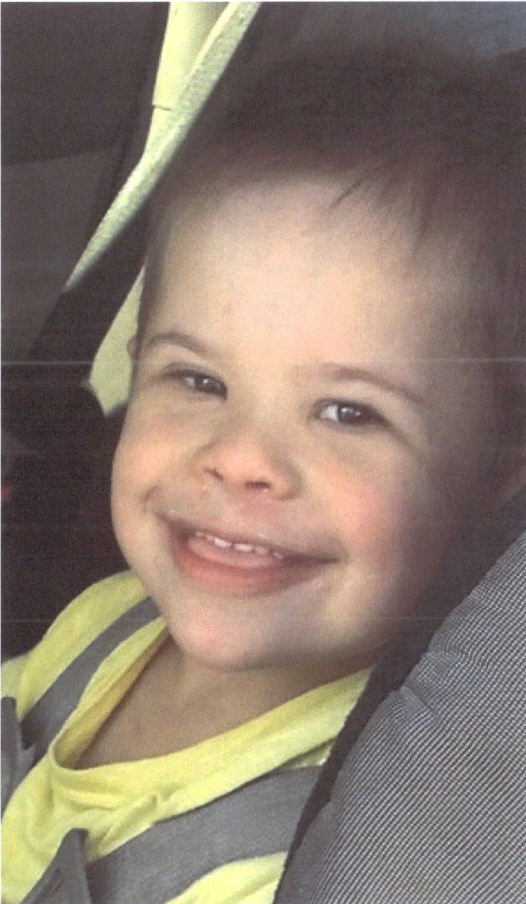

A PORTION OF THE PROCEEDS OF THIS BOOK ARE GOING TO NATIONAL DOWN SYNDROME SOCIETY.

My name is Cody, and I am 5 years old. I would like to tell you about my life. I have a mom and dad, one brother, two great-grandfathers, six grandmas and grandpas, and many aunts, uncles, and cousins.

When we are all together at
Christmas, there are 100 of us
in Dad's family, and they
all live near us.

Sometimes other kids make fun of me.
I don't pay any attention to them.
Mommy and Grandma tell me that they
were sometimes made fun of when they
were little too. I don't understand why
kids do that.

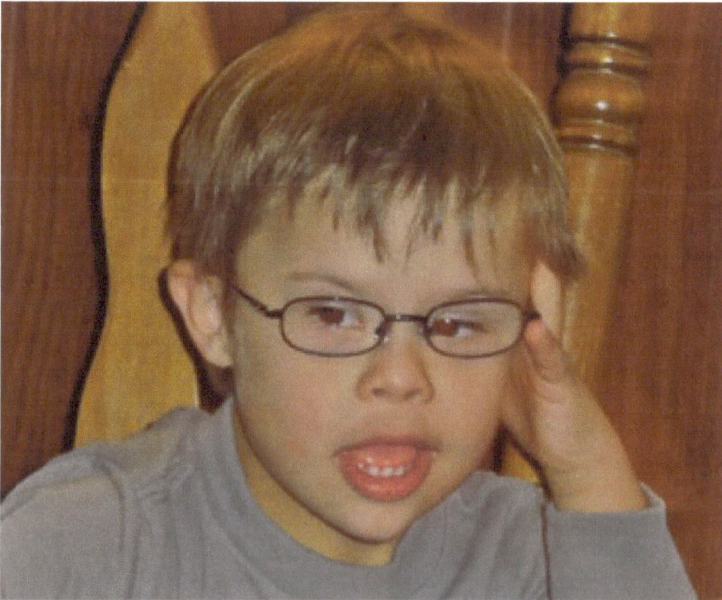

I hear I have Down syndrome,
and they say I have special needs.
Next fall, I will be in kindergarten in a
special education class part of the day.
I don't know what that means, but I know
that I am special because mommy and
daddy tell me I am.

Do you know what one of my favorite things is?

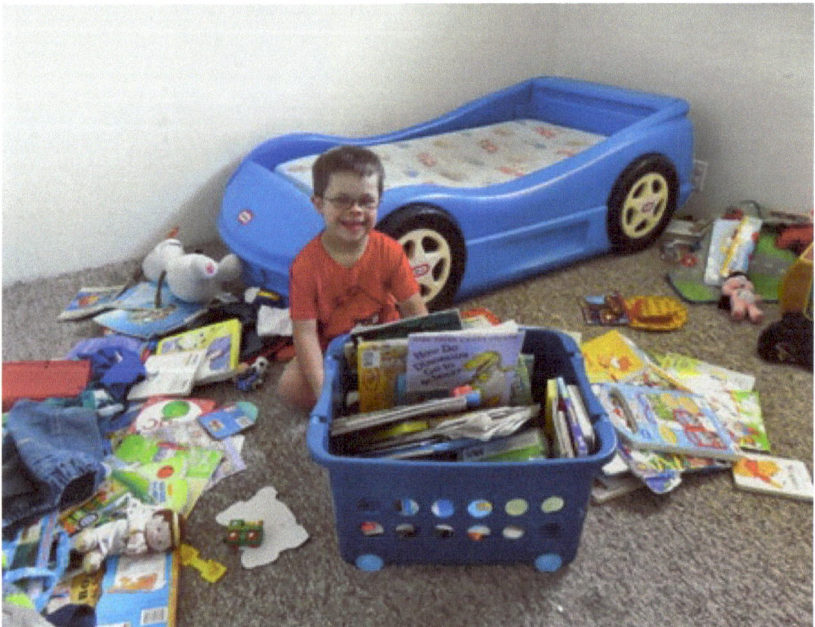

Books!!! I learn from them. My favorites are about farm animals, especially cows.

We have 12 goats at our home.
My brother, Jeremy, likes to
feed them.

Last night one of the goats had a baby.
We were all excited.
The baby goat is so cute.

I also like to swim in our big pool. Mommy has a unicorn float. I have never seen a real unicorn. Mommy likes them.

I love school. Each day I take the bus. As soon as I get on the bus, I take off my shoes and take a nap...on the way to school and on the way home.

Every Sunday we go to church, and I like the loud praise band. I try to play the drums when no one is watching. Everyone is happy to see me.

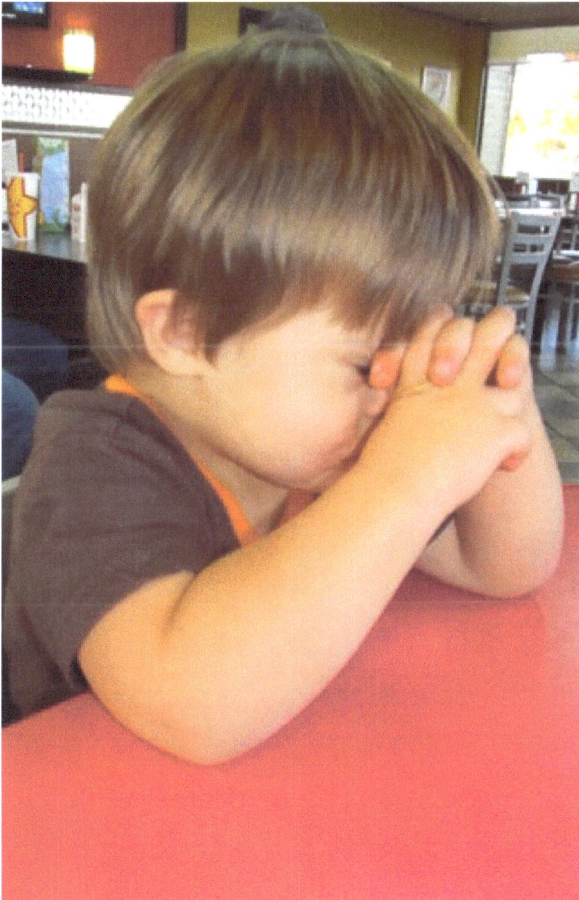

I always pray before we eat.

Climbing is lots of fun for me to do...in my yard, at the park, or anywhere.

Sometimes in my family, everyone talks at the same time, and it gets loud. One time I held up my hand and said, "Trying to talk." They thought that was very funny as they are always trying to get me to talk more.

I like to throw things...balls, shoes,
or anything...in the water or anywhere.
I was throwing things in my bedroom, and
Mommy came in and asked me, "Cody, what
are you doing?" Her voice was different
than it usually is. I said to myself,
"IN TROUBLE!"

When others don't understand
what I want, I bury my head on the floor
and feel bad. However, I have learned the
words that I need most, such as "Orange
juice," "Mine," and "No way." I also love
water...lots of water.

One thing I don't like is birthday candles. I used to cry when everyone sang "Happy Birthday" to me. It took my family a long time to figure out it was the fire on the candles that scared me.

See...no candles.

I like school and all the fun things we do there, especially the singing. We just had preschool graduation, where we did a program for our families. I get nervous when there is a change, like when I heard the families were coming to our school. I was too shy to sing and was just holding onto my teacher. She is really nice.

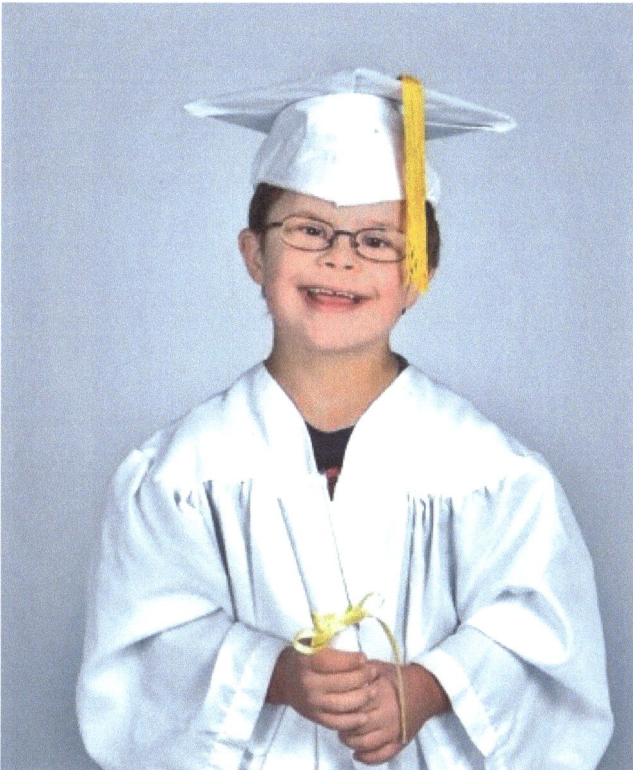

When I was given a balloon, I forgot that I was shy and had fun again.

I just started wearing glasses.
They hurt my nose, so I take them off
and set them down....anywhere. They often
get lost. One time I put them in a drain
pipe outside at my school. My nice teacher
spent an hour trying to get them out.
She did!

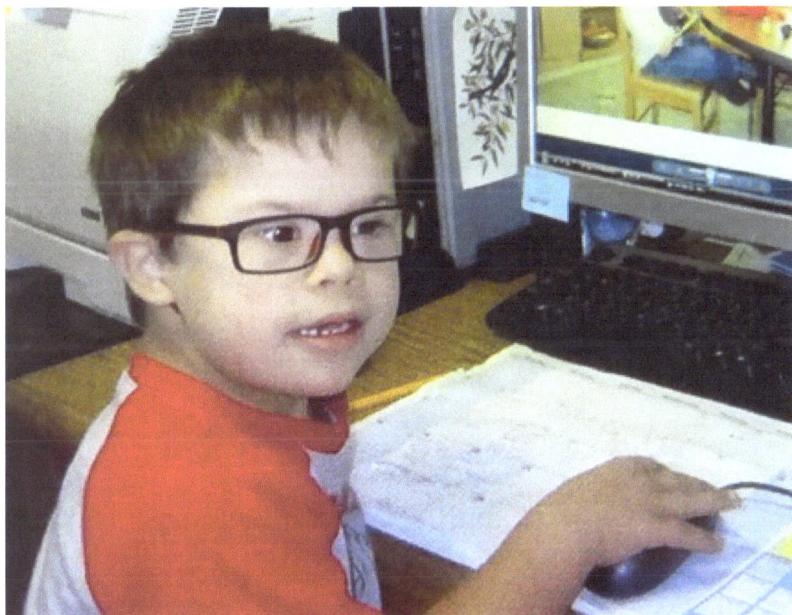

I love to twirl socks, towels, beads, or ribbon. Mommy and Daddy don't know why I like to do this. It just feels good and is fun for me.

I really like pirates and pirate ships. They are lots of fun!

I also like to pretend that I am Jake, the pirate.

They say I am funny. I do like to make people laugh.

Did you notice my socks?

This is Sherman. I think he eats too much. I used to pull his tail, but now I have learned to be nice to him.

My brother, Jeremy, and I play together a lot. Most of the time, he is good to me. Sometimes, though, he doesn't want to share with me.

I like to help clean off the table and help with clothes that have been washed. I always put things away that I play with. Jeremy doesn't. I also push my chair in after sitting at the table. Jeremy doesn't. I like to give everyone hugs. Jeremy doesn't.

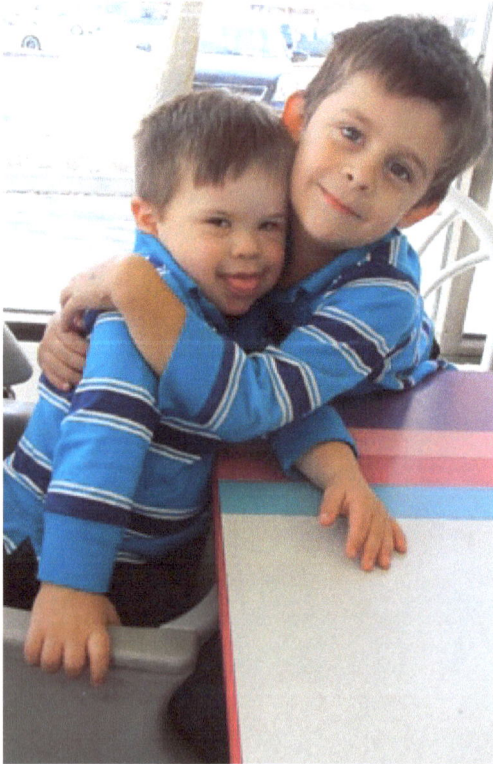

But sometimes he likes to hug me!

Life has its ups and downs. Most of the time I am up. Sometimes I feel on top of the world!

I have a fun life and am a very happy boy. Now you know about me and what I like and don't like. If I met you, I'm sure that I would like you.

Mommy and Daddy told me I was born with something called "an extra chromosome." They say that extra one is what gives me extra love for everyone.

ABOUT THE FAMILY

Jeremy and Cody live with their parents in the Sacramento area, and the family is active in Down syndrome support groups.

ABOUT THE AUTHOR

Dianne Flynn is married to Pastor Alan
Flynn, and they live in the Sacramento area.
Mrs. Flynn is the proud grandmother of
Cody and Jeremy. She has also written
My Brother's Ups and Downs.

My Life With Ups and Downs

ISBN: 978-0-692-77008-5

DiggyPOD Printing

Book orders can be placed at diannelouiseflynn@ gmail, Amazon, and on Facebook at My Life With Ups and Downs

Photos taken by Dianne Flynn
Page 2 photo taken by Joanne Hintz
Page 16 photo taken by Lifetouch
Pages 17 and 18 photos taken by Hillsdale Preschool
Page 28 taken by Kristin Hintz

www.ingramcontent.com/pod-product-compliance
Lightning Source LLC
Chambersburg PA
CBHW041759040426
42447CB00001B/29